Fig. 1

William de Leftwich Dodge, New York City, March 31, 1897, on his wedding day

EXHIBITION ITINERARY

Heckscher Museum of Art
Huntington, New York
June 20 – August 30, 1998

Telfair Museum of Art
Savannah, Georgia
September 15 – November 1, 1998

WILLIAM DE LEFTWICH DODGE

Impressions Home and Abroad

With Sculpture by Frederick William MacMonnies

April 10 – June 5, 1998

Essay by Ronald G. Pisano

BEACON HILL FINE ART

980 MADISON AVENUE, NEW YORK, NEW YORK 10021 TEL: 212.734.3636

William de Leftwich Dodge
Introduction

William de Leftwich Dodge is best remembered for his work as a muralist for important buildings such as the Library of Congress and the State House in Albany and for magnificent edifices at the Columbian Exposition and Panama-Pacific Exposition. Mural commissions were financially profitable and brought the artist considerable public recognition. However, Dodge's professional career was much more encompassing and versatile. His early work focused upon historical, grand-scale paintings, some painted for the Paris Salon; allegorical and religious subjects; and portraits. He also supplemented his earnings by working as an illustrator. Most noteworthy were his Impressionist oils and watercolors.

This exhibition features the less familiar aspects of the artist's oeuvre, his easel paintings. Studying in Paris, training with Gérôme, spending time in Giverny, and working at the Tenth Street Studio Building, Dodge was among all the important artists of his day, both American and European. These influences, along with his own talent, afforded him the opportunity to exhibit regularly and to develop close relationships. Frederick William MacMonnies, for example, painted his portrait and gave Dodge one of his most famous bronzes, *Pan of Rohallion*. Because of the close connection between the two artists, we have chosen to include a sampling of MacMonnies' sculptures among Dodge's paintings in the exhibition.

A highlight of this show is the recent discovery of a missing masterpiece, *The Death of Minnehaha*, painted in Paris (1885-1887), before the artist turned twenty. Inspired by Henry Wadsworth Longfellow's *The Song of Hiawatha*, this extraordinary canvas features a young French model as the maiden Minnehaha on her deathbed. Hiawatha and Nokomis (his grandmother), modeled after Native Americans performing at the time in Buffalo Bill's Wild West Show in Paris, weep at her bedside. Upon completion, the painting was sent to New York for the Prize Fund Exhibition of the American Art Association where it won a gold medal and cash award. The painting was also shown on several occasions in the United States at various art festivals and was often used as inspiration for living tableaux.

Minnehaha or "Laughing Water" was the wife of Hiawatha. Her name was derived from the "Little Falls," forty feet in height, on a stream emptying into the Mississippi River between Fort Snelling and the Falls of St. Anthony in Minnesota. The picture was appropriately purchased by a wealthy Midwestern family who eventually took it to Berlin where it inspired Hugo Kaun to write his symphonic poem about Hiawatha published in 1902.

Dodge's work includes his rare views of the South which resulted from trips to Savannah in 1905-1907 and 1928, and to the Mississippi Delta in 1933. Paintings range from his tonal *Georgia* or *Live Oak at Sunset* to his vibrantly painted *Summer Day Under Spanish Moss*. Figurative subjects were drawn from local inhabitants; one of his daughter and her nurse, *Sarah et Tante Katy*, was exhibited at the Paris Salon in 1907.

Much of Dodge's oeuvre is devoted to paintings of his grand estate, Villa Francesca, a Greek Revival mansion at Setauket, Long Island, built in 1906. Views of the villa include well-appointed interiors of the house, its lush gardens including an elaborate pergola, and its vast outlook onto the sea and surrounding terrain. The artist was infatuated with different times of day as in *The Gate*, and with various seasons as represented in *Upper Terrace*, *The Artist's Garden*, and *Dolphin Bay*. During this period, his daughter Sara or "Sally" figured prominently. *Sally Among the Irises* features the tow-headed young girl amidst luxuriant purple blossoms, while *Before the Ball* shows the ingenue jauntily posed in her yellow gown.

In this exhibition, the majority of Dodge's European subjects relates to the family's stay in Giverny, where they lived next to MacMonnies between 1898 and 1900, and to later travels to Sicily, southern Italy, and France between 1926 and 1928. *Woman on Garden Bench* (1898) is representative of the artist's predilection for painting his wife during this time. The artist's later watercolors (gouaches), *Deck of the SS De Grasse*, *Fountain of Medici*, and *Temple of Neptune, Paestum*, show a glimpse of Dodge's peripateticism and his proficiency in this medium.

Beacon Hill Fine Art is extremely grateful to Leftwich Dodge Kimbrough, the artist's grandson, and his wife Ursula for their generosity in allowing us to mount this exhibition. The Kimbroughs have been the caretakers not only of important works by the artist, but also of the preservation of his name and reputation. Through their efforts, we have been able to locate and display paintings relevant to our perspective as well as to illustrate photographs of the artist, his home, and his family. In particular, Leftwich's knowledge and editorial assistance have been invaluable in producing this catalogue. He indeed has made William de Leftwich Dodge come alive.

Ronald G. Pisano has mastered an extraordinary essay which will enlighten art historians and collectors for many years to come. His placement of Dodge within the context of his peers enhances our understanding of the artist and his importance, not only as a muralist, but also as a fine easel painter. On short order, Ron has made what would seem an overwhelming task easy and pleasurable.

We thank Robert Bardin for synthesizing Dodge's entire career into an interesting and informative chronology. D. Frederick Baker, through his editing skills, perseverance, and support, has been invaluable in producing this catalogue. We especially appreciate the interest of the two institutions on our exhibition itinerary and particularly, the enthusiasm of Anne Cohen DePietro, Curator of the Heckscher Museum of Art, Huntington, New York, and Diane Lesko, Director, and Chris Neal, Curator, of the Telfair Museum of Art, Savannah, Georgia. The extension of the show to museum venues is truly rewarding.

There are many colleagues in the field who have given their time, knowledge, and effort to both loans and content: H. Barbara Weinberg, Curator of Paintings and Sculpture, The Metropolitan Museum of Art; Martha Severens, Curator, and Claudia Beckwith, Registrar, Greenville County Museum of Art; Elizabeth Broun, Director, and Abigail Terrones, Associate Registrar, National Museum of American Art; Robert MacKay, Director, Society for the Preservation of Long Island Antiquities; and David Park Curry, Chief Curator, Virginia Museum of Fine Arts.

Finally, we are grateful to the many private lenders, both anonymous and listed. We would especially like to thank Janis Conner, Frederick Hill, James Berry Hill, David Knoke, Betty Krulik, M.P. Naud, Ira Spanierman, Joel Rosenkranz, and Steve Tatti for making this exhibition meaningful. And, a special note of appreciation must be given to Jane Egan for organizing the MacMonnies sculptures and Dodge photographs, and for editorial support; to Catherine Miller Penn for coordinating the loans and checklist; to Peter Ramon for preparing the works for this major exhibition; and to Dan Dyksen for an even more creative catalogue design.

Debra J. Force, Director
April 1998

Fig. 2
Summer Day Under Spanish Moss, oil on canvas, 40 x 24 inches. Greenville County Museum of Art, Greenville, South Carolina; Museum purchase with funds provided by Alester G. Furman III, The Pellett Foundation, and The Museum Association, Inc.

PLATE 1
Frederick William MacMonnies, *Portrait of William de Leftwich Dodge*, circa 1898, oil on canvas, 23⅞ x 23⅞ inches.
Collection of Ms. Gretchen Carhartt Valade, Grosse Pointe Farms, Michigan

WILLIAM DE LEFTWICH DODGE
Impressions Home and Abroad

When William de Leftwich Dodge died, March 25, 1935, The New York Times referred to him as "one of the country's outstanding mural painters...a leader in his field."[1] On a more personal note, the celebrated American sculptor Frederick MacMonnies lamented the loss of a "loyal friend" who had a "zest for living" as well as a fine appreciation for "all the beautiful aspects of life."[2] When Dodge designed some of the nation's most important and grand-scale murals, celebrating the history, culture, and spirit of the United States, he had a simple underlying scheme in mind, explaining, "While some of my work may seem elaborate, my chief aim is for simplicity."[3] This philosophy is better seen in his less well-known easel paintings and watercolors which are of a more personal nature. Whether views of the walled-in garden of the house he rented in Giverny, France (1898-1900), or the interiors of the magnificent home he designed for his family in 1906, Villa Francesca, high on sand bluffs overlooking Smithtown Bay in Setauket, Long Island, these works bespeak a quiet, simple, artfully composed life dedicated to creating art.

Born March 9, 1867, in Liberty (later renamed Bedford), Virginia, to Mary Leftwich and William M. Dodge, William de Leftwich Dodge had a somewhat eccentric and peripatetic upbringing, moving for the first time at the age of two when the family relocated to Chicago.[4] His mother, known as "Mamie," a strong-willed woman with artistic aspirations, descended from an old Virginia family; his father, an insurance agent, was originally from New York. William was the second of three children: he had an older sister, Anita, and a younger brother, Robert. Some time in 1879, when William was twelve, the Dodges moved from Chicago to Brooklyn, New York; but, before the year was out, Mamie took her three children and left for Europe. Just what arrangements she made with her husband, who was left behind and never reunited with his family, remain a mystery. Apparently Mamie believed that there were better opportunities for her artistic career on the Continent; and according to at least one source, she achieved some degree of success in Munich, where she and her children spent a year in 1880.[5] William and his siblings had barely begun to learn German when she decided to move to Paris, and they turned their attention to French. William recalled a rather frugal existence in their small flat at 33 rue de Moscou, where Mamie encouraged the fourteen-year-old to study art. After yet another move in 1882, this time to 3 rue d'Alençon, William began his formal training, drawing plaster casts from the Antique in the morning at the Ecole des Beaux-Arts and in the evening at the Académie Colarossi.[6]

While at Colarossi's, Dodge met another American art student, Frederick MacMonnies, who would become a lifelong friend and one of America's most accomplished sculptors. In fact, Dodge informed MacMonnies of the free drawing class at the Ecole, which met six mornings a week and benefited from the twice-weekly criticisms of the renowned French Academician, Jean Léon Gérôme. Dodge was so impressed by the French master that he became determined to enter into his atelier, gaining entrance as an unmatriculated student in 1883. To enroll formally as a matriculated student at the Ecole, he would have to pass a rigorous exam that demonstrated proof of his proficiency in drawing as well as answering difficult questions relating to history and other academic subjects. Competition was keen. "The number of admissions at a professor's disposal in the Beaux-Arts is limited by the mere area of the place, while the applicants are

FIG. 3
William de Leftwich Dodge, circa 1914

virtually without number," explained one student.[7] Despite these odds, Dodge confidently took his examination in 1883, at age sixteen, but failed.

Although American students considered it a great honor to be admitted to the Ecole, many could not pass the rigid examination and chose the Académie Julian, a private school founded by one of the Ecole's former pupils, Rodolphe Julian. The daily procedure was pretty much the same, the major difference being that there were no entrance examinations; also there was a nominal fee whereas the Ecole was free. Although Dodge had financial constraints, it is doubtful that it was the fee that deterred him from choosing this alternative; he had made up his mind to study under Gérôme and he intended to persist until he passed the test. His efforts, however, were disrupted when an epidemic of Asiatic cholera broke out in Paris in 1884, and he and his family were forced to flee the city, finding refuge in Berlin.[8] There, Dodge took classes at the Königliche Akademische Hochschule, where he excelled and won an award.

After six months, instilled with even greater confidence, Dodge returned to Paris and attempted the Ecole's examination a second time — and failed again. It was not until his sixth try, after two frustrating years, that Dodge finally passed the matriculation exam on April 4, 1885, placing number one on the list of inductees. Later in life he told his daughter that "...success comes only through long, conscientious application," — a lesson he had well learned and later put to good use.[9] For the next four years he painted under Gérôme's watchful eye and guiding spirit, winning various prizes including two third-class medals, two honorable mentions, and ultimately the coveted Prix d'Atelier (first-class medal).

Even after being admitted to Gérôme's atelier, Dodge's struggle did not cease, as he recalled, "The first week I studied under Gérôme he told me I would better have stayed in my own savage country and planted cabbages than to have come to Paris to study drawing."[10] After delivering such harsh criticism, Gérôme was surprised to see Dodge return to class

the following week, and apologized, but then assured his student his criticism was leveled at him for his own good. In a eulogy written after Gérôme's death, Dodge recounted: "It was not always 'très bien' with him...we more often heard 'mauvais' ringing out when he was correcting his class. No one could be a harsher or more severe critic than he."[11] On the other hand, the American painter Julian Alden Weir, also a Gérôme student, recalled "...the care and attention which he gave to all his pupils."[12] Most important, Weir credited his mentor as being a great artist who commanded great respect. The American painter Douglas Volk, another student of Gérôme, concurred, asserting: "I doubt if any master of our times was held in greater reverence by his pupils than Gérôme."[13] Enthusiastically, Volk conjured up the effect created by Gérôme, the "overpowering awe," as he entered the Ecole for his regular critiques: "A state of pandemonium often reigned supreme among the forest of easels that choked this historical place...But when, at the appointed time, the great door of the studio opened softly and Gérôme entered what a sudden stillness fell on that crowd of restless workers! Then did all wait reverently on his every word."[14]

It is no wonder that Dodge strove relentlessly to achieve a position in this class. Talk in the studio often drifted to some of Gérôme's earlier American students, who by this time had already become celebrated artists in their own right; in addition to Weir and Volk, there were George de Forest Brush and Thomas Eakins. A contemporary article describes the abuse newly inducted students, like Dodge, had to endure at the Ecole — especially the Americans - each "nouveau" was directed to run errands, wash brushes, and purchase refreshments. Only then would their fellow students drink "to the health of George Washington."[15] Americans were also the butt of jokes about their "savage" country; when an American student accidently broke out in English, one of the Parisian students rebuked in French: "We don't speak Iroquois!"[16]

For his first major composition Dodge chose a Native American subject, *The Death of Minnehaha*, 1887 (Fig. 5), from Henry Wadsworth Longfellow's poem, "The Song of Hiawatha," first published in America in 1855.[17] Longfellow was praised for choosing this subject, a truly American theme, when other American poets were drawing their inspiration from Europe. Fifty thousand copies were sold in the first two years after publication; and although interest had diminished during the Civil War, there was a revival afterward, which lasted into the 1880s. Subjects from the poem appealed particularly to artists who had probably read the work during their youth — among them the painters Thomas Moran,

FIG. 4
Study for the Death of Minnehaha, circa 1887, charcoal on paper, 18½ x 41¼ inches

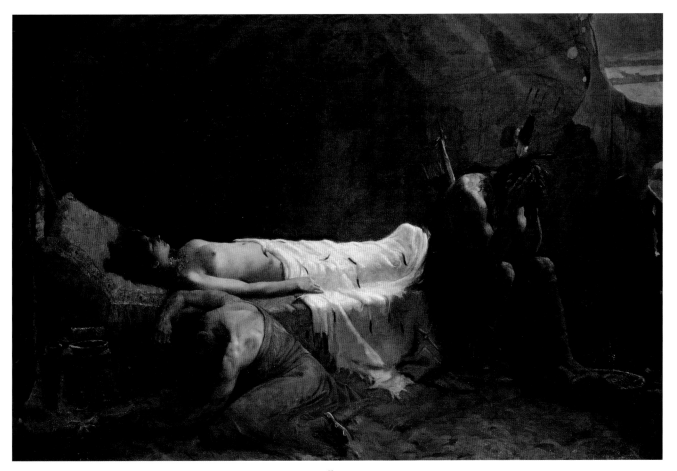

FIG. 5
The Death of Minnehaha, 1887, oil on canvas, 77 x 121 inches

Albert Bierstadt, and Thomas Eakins, and the sculptors Edmonia Lewis and Augustus Saint-Gaudens. Dodge's painting, begun in 1885, was the latest among these works, but achieved the most notable success. This may be attributed to several factors including its grand scale. Dodge had originally intended to debut this ambitious painting at the Paris Salon, and had requested permission to charge his art materials to his mother's account at Paul Foinet's art supply shop. Although overextended with bills of her own, Mamie allowed him to do so. Apparently it was this need for funds that caused Dodge to change his course of action upon completion of the work. Instead of submitting it to the Salon (where there were no cash awards), he sent it to New York to be entered in the Prize Fund Exhibition of 1887. To his delight it was awarded one of ten gold medals and an accompanying $300 award. The finished painting and a large study (Fig. 4) for its main figure attest to Dodge's mastery of rendering the human figure in the manner of his mentor, Gérôme.

When *The Death of Minnehaha* was shown in New York, the fact that it was painted in the tradition of the Paris Salon did not go unnoticed, with one critic observing that Dodge had "...caught the prevailing Paris fashion of large canvases."[18]

Having sacrificed his first major exhibition piece to America, Dodge made his debut at the Paris Salon in 1887 with a bas-relief sculpture, *Portrait of Mlle. XXX*. Dodge's entry in the 1888 Salon was a monumental canvas, *David (David and Goliath)*, produced specifically for exhibition purposes and executed in the historically accurate and highly finished manner of Gérôme. By this point, Dodge had clearly mastered the Salon formula and was placed high within the ranks of American artists who, by the mid-1880s, had become the largest foreign group in Paris, gaining strength each year as they competed in the Salon exhibitions and in other important international shows.[19] When the Exposition Universelle was held in Paris in 1889, the American artists' display was the largest of all foreign exhibitors; and in the category of painting alone, they were awarded two grand prizes, four gold medals, fourteen silver medals, and thirty-eight bronze medals. Dodge, the youngest artist represented in the exhibition, was one of the bronze medal winners for his painting, *David and Goliath* (shown previously at the Paris Salon of 1888).[20] In fact, the connection between Americans who won prizes at the Exposition Universelle and who exhibited at the Salon was amazingly strong: all of the winners of gold and silver medals

4

had been Salon participants. Dodge showed at the Salon regularly for over a decade.

In the fall of 1889, after nearly ten years abroad, Dodge decided to return to New York City, probably prompted by the recent success of his paintings *The Death of Minnehaha* and *David and Goliath*, which were widely publicized in the American press. In New York he shared a studio with a former classmate from the Ecole, George Bridgman, at 4 and 6 West Fourteenth Street (probably adjoining spaces). The following year he showed three paintings at the annual exhibition of the National Academy of Design.[21] In December 1890, sixty-nine of Dodge's works were shown in a group exhibition held at the American Art Association in New York; the other artists were Charles Walter Stetson and Alexander Harrison. Of the three, Harrison was by far the most established painter, particularly well respected by American artists working in Paris, where he had achieved considerable acclaim at the Salon. As a means of establishing his own importance, Dodge made sure to feature his Salon successes and other prize winning paintings in this joint show, listing them first in the catalogue, along with notations about their prizes.[22] The remainder of his paintings were portraits, landscapes, figures, and "decorations." Little is known of any of these works, many of which were probably destroyed by a fire in the artist's studio the following year. However, judging from their titles, they appear to have been done over the previous several years in France. Based on one of the landscapes that has survived, *Sunset* (1888), it is evident that Dodge had already developed a personal style in his plein-air paintings, combining the tonal palette and evocative mood of the French Barbizon painters with the more stark naturalism of the French Realist, Jules Bastien-Lepage.[23] The titles of Dodge's other paintings in the exhibit suggest a growing interest in various effects of sunlight as he began exploring a more Impressionist style of painting, while not totally abandoning his Academic training.[24]

The route that Dodge traveled in forging his own style of Impressionism was indirect and inconsistent. His earliest known attempt along these lines, *Water Lilies. Girl in Sunlight*, circa 1888, was clearly influenced by the work of the American expatriate artist Alexander Harrison. Harrison, a close friend of Bastien-Lepage, had achieved considerable recognition, especially among artists, for the success of his painting *En Arcadie*. Portraying several nude women posed out-of-doors, it was featured in the Salon of 1886. Close on the heals of Harrison's success was Dodge's painting *Water Lilies. Girl in Sunlight*, depicting a nude woman reclining on the grass and dipping her hair into a pool, which was given the honor of being hung "on the line" (at eye level) in the Salon of 1889. Although Harrison had established the mode for Dodge and other American painters who achieved critical acclaim in France for this subject, many American art critics objected to these works. When Dodge's painting was featured in the joint show of 1890, one conservative member of the press facetiously described it as a "...nude individual...trying to stand on her head in a stagnant pool."[25] And when this painting and Harrison's *En Arcadie* were shown at the annual exhibition of

Fig. 6
Isis in the Marshes of the Nile, 1897, oil on canvas, 20 x 39½ inches

PLATE 2
Woman on a Garden Bench (The Artist's Wife in Giverny), 1898, oil on canvas, 31½ x 21½ inches. Private Collection, Arkansas

the Pennsylvania Academy of the Fine Arts in 1891, they were accorded little more respect. One critic attacked their "mere nakedness," preferring the more sentimental nudes of Kenyon Cox and Will H. Low who toned down their subjects with allegorical and classical references.[26] This negative reaction to Dodge's more progressive work would continue to plague him.

Anxious to raise much needed funds at a time when his paintings had little market value, Dodge turned to illustration. He also traveled to Chicago in 1891, attempting to obtain a mural commission for the upcoming World's Columbian Exposition. Although unsuccessful in his initial attempt, he managed to get work (along with ten other artists) painting a large cyclorama of the Chicago Fire of 1871. Ironically, as he was completing work on this project, he received word that his own studio in New York City had suffered a bad fire and he returned home immediately. Depressed but determined, Dodge learned that there was one mural commission for the Columbian Exposition that had not yet been awarded, and he directed his full energy to securing this work. The mural, *The Glorification of the Arts and Sciences*, was for the dome of the Administration Building. Designed by the architect Richard Morris Hunt, this building was to be the tallest structure at the fair with a dome of 315 feet in circumference by 50-feet deep. Unintimidated, the audacious artist, then twenty-four, approached Hunt directly and managed to win his approval.

FIG. 7
William de Leftwich Dodge behind Frederick MacMonnies,
River Epte, Giverny, circa 1898

Securing this coveted commission proved to be a major turning point in Dodge's life and was certainly uplifting to his spirits. It did not however go without complications; only $3,000 was allotted for the project, barely enough for the paint, and construction was behind schedule.[27] His brother Robert, also trained at the Beaux Arts, came over from Paris to assist in the project.

In the meantime, an auction of ninety-six of Dodge's recent paintings, including some that had either survived the studio fire or had been stored elsewhere, was held in New York at the Fifth Avenue Art Galleries (Oct. 27-28, 1892). Commenting on their Impressionistic style, one critic observed: "They are facile, well-lighted and brilliantly colored pictures with a strong decorative quality."[28] And while objecting to the "uncompromising realism" in Dodge's nudes, one writer praised them for their vigorous quality, singling out his *Water Lilies. Girl in Sunlight* as one of the most important works shown.[29] Although the auction was only a limited success, the sale and his mural commission provided enough money for savings and investment. Unfortunately, 1893 turned out to be the onset of an economic depression in the United States, and Dodge, who had lost most of his money, returned to New York nearly penniless.

After several calamitous years in America, Dodge decided to return to Paris in 1894. Financial opportunities were very limited there, but accommodations were less expensive and critics were more appreciative of his art. He resumed exhibiting at the Salon and sent these paintings back to the United States for important exhibitions in Philadelphia and Chicago. When several were shown in Chicago in 1895, one writer declared: "There is no American artist of the day who has been more talked about."[30] His greatest success at this time, however, was based mainly on another major mural commission, this one destined for the northwest corner pavilion of the Library of Congress, a large ceiling design (25 by 25 feet), *Ambition*, and four tympanums, *Literature, Music, Science,* and *Art* (each 10 by 35 feet).[31] Overjoyed at being recognized by the Government of his native land, the commission (reported to be $8000) enabled him to achieve greater economic security. After two years of work on his murals and the exhibition of its center panel in the Salon of 1896, Dodge prepared, with renewed enthusiasm, to return home to New York that fall. Before delivering his murals to Washington, DC, for installation, he showed them, along with their studies and various easel paintings at the American Art Association Galleries in New York, beginning November 2, 1896. Portraits, figure paintings, and landscapes of France and

Austria were among the sixty works featured. Also included were marines and a few studies for his Salon paintings.

As a means of capitalizing on his recent success in obtaining mural commissions, Dodge scheduled an auction of fifty-three of his paintings at the Fifth Avenue Art Galleries in New York, February, 1897. Also included were fifty-two drawings for his Library of Congress murals. The preview for this sale was held concurrently with an exhibition of the work of J. Alden Weir. Dodge must have been pleased with this coincidental association with the well-respected American painter, especially when one critic linked them as painters of the "modern school of impressionism in France...without losing their own vigor and originality."[32] The same writer declared the auction exhibition of Dodge's work to be the "cleverest one man show of the art season."[33]

Some confusion was generated, however, by the fact that Dodge exhibited paintings of such variant styles side by side. Reaction to Dodge's Impressionistic easel paintings was generally negative as critics continued to prefer his highly finished exhibition pieces done under the influence of Gérôme rather than the more casual and freely painted plein-air figure pieces. Furthermore, as his reputation grew, based almost exclusively on the success of his mural paintings, critics could not understand or fully appreciate the directness of his Impressionist paintings, which by comparison, seemed to lack poetry, grandeur, and symbolic or narrative detail. The results of the auction were described as "fairly successful," with fifty-three of the paintings averaging $100 apiece. The highest prices achieved were, not surprisingly, for Dodge's major exhibition pieces, still favored by the conservative public: *Diana* ($400); *Evening Dance* ($800); and *Dream of Orpheus* ($800).[34] The sale still raised a considerable amount of money and added to Dodge's financial stability.

On March 31, 1897, William de Leftwich Dodge married Frances Theodora Bland Pryor. Fanny, the daughter of Sara and Roger A. Pryor, was a distant cousin of Dodge's. Her father had been a prominent United States Congressman from Virginia who lost everything in the Civil War, but reestablished himself in New York where he practiced law and became a state supreme court justice. Dodge had courted Fanny over five years, but because of previous unstable finances had not been able to ask for her hand. Her high social standing was underscored by the long list of prominent guests who attended the wedding as reported in the society column of <u>The New York Times</u>, including: Mr. and Mrs. John D. Rockefeller, President [of Columbia University] and Mrs. Seth Low, Mr. and Mrs. Robert E. Lee Lewis, and Mr. and Mrs.

Spencer Trask. Missing from this list were members of Dodge's immediate family. For the couple's honeymoon, the Trasks provided their country home, "Yaddo," in Saratoga Springs, New York, where the newlyweds spent a week before traveling abroad on April 10 to Italy, southern France, and ultimately Paris, where they planned to reside.[35]

Dodge returned to his studio at 9 rue des Fourneaux and rented an apartment at the Place du Crosic, where the couple's son Roger was born the following year. Evidently, Dodge had some trouble adjusting to fatherhood, and was having difficulty with an exhibition piece he was preparing for the Salon. So, in March 1898 he decided to take a brief trip to Algiers for a rest, accompanied by his friend MacMonnies and the

FIG. 8
Frederick MacMonnies,
Admonishing Cupid,
bronze, 16¼ inches high

sculptor's student, Paul Conkling.[36] Dodge confided his problems to MacMonnies who suggested he spend the summer in Giverny, just forty miles northwest of Paris. MacMonnies had discovered the small art colony in 1890, and in 1893 he began summering there regularly. Among the first American painters to visit Giverny were Alexander Harrison, who made frequent trips there as early as 1888, and Theodore Robinson.

Will H. Low, who visited Robinson in Giverny the summer of 1892, later recalled his first impression of the town: "Giverny, as a hamlet struggling along an unshaded road, offers at first glance little that is picturesque."[37] Low soon found, however, that the setting had a subtle beauty: "Through the valley which it dominates runs the Seine, and between the village and the larger river winds a small stream, the Epte, with pleasantly shaded banks enclosed between broad meadows gracefully bordered by long lines of poplars."[38] Low also claimed that the village had become overrun by American painters, particularly women students, and that the resident celebrity, Claude Monet, took refuge from the marauders "behind the gates of his beautiful garden."[39] The French Impressionist kept pretty much to himself and made virtually no attempt to offer advice. "The tenets of the so-called Impressionists forbid the relation of pupil to master," Low

FIG. 9
The Music Lesson, Giverny, 1900, oil on panel, 11¾ x 52 inches. Private Collection, Chevy Chase, Maryland

explained, their motto being "nature seen through individual temperament."[40] The other artists in the colony, however, were abuzz with technical jargon: "color values," "vibration," "decomposition of tones," and "orange light and purple shadows."[41]

By the time the Dodges arrived in the summer of 1898, things had quieted down considerably. Alexander Harrison had made his last visit there the spring of the preceding year, and Frederick MacMonnies and his painter wife, Mary Fairchild MacMonnies, were the dominant figures among the American colonists.[42] During their first visit in April 1890, the MacMonnieses stayed at the Hôtel Baudy, a popular haunt for foreign visitors. They became regular summer residents after several visits in 1893, taking a three-year lease on Villa

FIG. 10
Figaro Illustré, 1899, oil on canvas, 36 x 28¾ inches.
Collection of Ursula and Leftwich Dodge Kimbrough

Besche where they created a lovely garden that served as the setting for many of Mary's paintings. The Dodges rented a quaint one-story house on the edge of the village, surrounded by a stone wall, creating, in effect, an outdoor studio. Riding back and forth to the village on a tandem bicycle, William and Fanny often passed Monet painting, but having been forewarned about his intolerance of intruders, they left him undisturbed. Among the other artists there at the time were Theodore Robinson and a coterie of MacMonnies students: Paul and Mabel Conkling and Rosina and "Bay" (Ellen) Emmet.

Although Dodge had taken up plein-air painting a decade earlier and had specialized in painting the figure, especially the female nude in a natural outdoor setting, he carried his technique a step further over the next three summers spent in Giverny. His paintings became diffused with light and atmosphere as he utilized broken color and fragmented brushwork, adopting Impressionist methods. During the summer of 1899, the Dodges stayed at the Hôtel Baudy but regularly visited the MacMonnieses who gave the painter ready access to their beautiful garden. With increasing financial success, the MacMonnieses moved to a three-acre estate, Le Prieure (The Priory), an abandoned three-century-old monastery on several acres, which became known as "MacMonastery." Its garden, which they carefully cultivated, became the envy of the colonists and was said to have rivaled Monet's in size and beauty. Mary MacMonnies painted at least two female nudes outdoors during this period, a subject treated on one occasion by her husband as well. And, although Dodge has been credited for popularizing this theme among the American artists in Giverny, they all would have been aware of Harrison's precedent, *En Arcadie*.

The third and last time the Dodges summered at Giverny, in 1900, was apparently spent in a rented cottage surrounded by a stone wall — perhaps the same cottage they had leased in 1898. In the privacy of his own modest garden, Dodge painted three outdoor nude subjects, using a model he had brought from Paris. Two of these paintings, *The Music Lesson, Giverny* (Fig. 9) and *Georgette in Giverny Garden*, nearly identical in size, have been described as "companion pictures." The first, in which a young male plays the pipes of pan for a young female companion is in the Arcadian tradition popularized by Kenyon Cox and Will H. Low. The second, a sensual reclining nude, is more closely related to similar Salon paintings popularized by the French Academics Alexandre Cabanel and William Bouguereau. The third painting, *La Sainte Ivresse*, also known as *Love's Awakening*, was actually conceived as a Salon painting; it was shown at the Salon of 1901. Compared to *The Music Lesson, Giverny* and *Georgette*, which are relatively relaxed and natural, *La Sainte Ivresse* is posed and sentimental. This was typical of Dodge's varying production as he moved to a Modern style but was unable to give up his hold on the Academic tradition in which he was trained. Each summer spent in Giverny he would paint plein-air landscapes and contemporary figure pieces, while much of the rest of the year would be devoted to manufacturing grand productions for the Salon that would then be sent back to the United States for exhibition.

While Dodge's grand-scale paintings, such as *The Last Days of Tenochtitlan* shown at the 1899 Salon, continued to attract attention from both French and American critics, they were beginning to be criticized as being outdated. And, in their adherence to acknowledged French Salon standards, they were attacked by some American critics as being too "foreign." Perhaps in reaction to this, Dodge began submitting works of a more personal nature and intimate scale to the Salon shows, such as his *Family Group* (Fig. 12) shown at the 1902 Salon.

Even before this point, Dodge realized that he had exhausted possibilities for adequate work in Paris. The illustrations he was doing for the Paris magazine Figaro (Fig. 10), provided much needed income, but it was not enough to support his needs. There seemed to be greater prospects back home. His friends George Bridgman and George Grey Barnard had returned to New York and assumed prominent teaching positions at the Art Students League. Dodge also had offers to do illustrations for American periodicals; and he was about to have a major one-man show in New York in 1900. Although originally planned as a temporary visit with Fanny's parents on West 69th Street, their stay in the United States became permanent with the birth of their daughter Sara the following year and with the prospect of lucrative mural commissions. They took a house at 155 East 79th Street, and Dodge rented a studio at 51 West Tenth Street in the

FIG. 11
Lady in Blue, circa 1917, gouache and pencil on paper, 13 x 9 inches.
Private Collection

popular Tenth Street Studio Building.

Dodge's solo exhibition was held at the American Art Galleries in December 1900 and then traveled to Chicago. As in past shows, the artist included a broad variety of subjects: landscapes, portraits, marines, allegorical subjects, illustrations, and several of his recent Salon productions. The size of the show, 135 works, was impressive, and the range of styles, from academically painted figure pieces to full-fledged impressionistic paintings, was overwhelming. Two magazine articles were devoted to the show and to Dodge's career, Art Education (February, 1901)[43] and Truth (March, 1901).[44] The writer for Art Education observed that previously Dodge's easel paintings had remained virtually unnoticed, overshadowed by his vast Salon canvases and murals. Finding a common thread, this astute critic summarized, "...it is all very European in spirit. For this reason it has not been understood by the art critics of the New York newspapers."[45]

Aside from the obvious and direct connection to France observed in Dodge's Salon paintings, there was a similar association detected in his nudes painted outdoors. Whereas the sophisticated writer for Art Education attributed an aesthetic value to these paintings, describing them as "beautiful harmonies," a "subtle blending of figure with foliage, field

PLATE 3
The Gate, Villa Francesca, circa 1910, oil on canvas, 25¼ x 18¼ inches. Private Collection, Ann Arbor, Michigan

PLATE 4
Upper Terrace, Villa Francesca, circa 1915, oil on canvas, 35 x 23 inches

FIG. 12
Family Group, 1901, oil on canvas, 48 x 48 inches

and sky,"[46] less sophisticated critics were aghast by what they considered to be lewdness and indecency. By the time the show reached Chicago in January 1901, critical outrage over this matter had peaked. The <u>Chicago Chronicle</u> reported that "a coterie of local art critics are holding up their hands in horror."[47] The Art Institute of Chicago was attacked for giving such objectionable paintings a place on their walls; the female officer of a local art society refused to be introduced to Dodge at the reception; and others complained that several paintings of the nude should be turned to the wall or withdrawn by the artist. One unfrazzled critic calmly retorted that those who objected obviously had not been "educated in the views of the Parisians and Italians as regards to high art," a counter-opinion that only fueled the flames.[48] Even Dodge's *The Eighth Olympiad, a Greek Festival, 748-745 B. C.*, just shown to great acclaim at the Salon of 1900 and featured in this show, was condemned as a "scene of debauchery," in which the women were portrayed as being drunk. This prompted one critic to examine carefully each and every figure and report that such an interpretation was invalid. Defending Dodge's nudes, the same writer claimed: "It is the art of the centuries with a new brush stroke and new color."[49] In spite of all this hoopla, there was considerable praise from serious art critics. Dodge was hailed as a great colorist and lauded for his dashing brushwork. One writer proclaimed the paintings to be "spectacular,"[50] another declared them "brilliant."[51] A third writer summarized: "This is all dashing work...he carries the spectator off his feet, and takes his breath away."[52]

Most important, the articles published on Dodge in <u>Art Education</u> and <u>Truth</u> introduced his easel paintings to the public and provided insight into his career in general. Each subject was carefully considered and sensitively analyzed. Although the writer for <u>Art Education</u> claimed that Dodge placed greater value on his figure pieces than on his marines and landscapes, this critic found the landscapes to be worthy of special attention. Undoubtedly, Dodge did these plein-air paintings mainly for his own pleasure, although he had shown several of them previously at the annual exhibitions of the Pennsylvania Academy of the Fine Arts and the Art Institute of Chicago. Few of these works have surfaced, but one might assume the landscapes were Impressionistic, sun-dappled scenes similar to the backgrounds in his outdoor figure pieces done in Giverny. The marines probably resembled *The Sea at East Hampton* (1902) which, in its dramatically horizontal format, tonal palette, and evocative mood, closely parallels the marines of Alexander Harrison. Harrison had set the standard for such work in the 1880s and 1890s with several Salon paintings.

Dodge, however, considered his portraiture to be not only of greater importance but a potential source of added income. Previous to this one-man show (1900/1901) which included not only family portraits but what might presumably be categorized as society portraits, Dodge had rarely shown portraits in major exhibitions. Dodge's personal portraits of family members, such as the one of his son *Roger*, attracted particular attention. And Dodge's intent in pursuing this line of work was soon made clear. His *Mother and Child*, which was debuted in the show, and praised for its casual pose and special quality of light, was immediately sent off to be shown at the 1901 Salon.[53] The following year he exhibited *Family Group*, portraying himself with his wife and two children, at the 1902 Salon. Special mention was given to these two works in an article on Dodge in the <u>Fine Arts Journal</u> (1903) in which *Family Group* was declared to be "one of the artist's latest triumphs...very individual in composition, as well as original in conception."[54] The critic directed the viewer to Dodge's particular skill in rendering his models' hands — the "bête noir" of most artists and declared the painting to be a "lovely work of art and a type which few American artists — more the pity — affect."[55] The article, which also featured a reproduction of Dodge's *Portrait of Miss Page Brown*, set the stage for his next one-man show, "Portraits and Paintings by William de Leftwich Dodge," held at the Durand-Ruel Galleries, New York, January 19-26, 1904.

The Durand-Ruel show consisted of thirty-two paintings,

three-quarters of which were portraits. Included were his *Mother and Child* shown at the Salon of 1901, *My Family (Family Group)* shown at the Salon of 1902, and *Miss Katrina Page Brown*, most likely the same portrait featured in the <u>Fine Arts Journal</u> article. There were portraits of his children, including *Baby Roger (Roger with Guitar)* and *Sara (The Blue Bow)*, and at least four of his in-laws, the Pryors. Also featured were portraits of colleagues: the sculptor Philip Martiny and the architect John Carrère. More notable were his commissioned society portraits of George M. Pullman (inventor of the railway sleeping car) and of Pullman's daughter, Mrs. Francis Carolan. Given the social connections of his father-in-law, Judge Roger A. Pryor, Dodge probably could have done very well in this line of work, but his experience in painting the portraits of Mr. Pullman and his daughter was so unnerving that he all but abandoned his pursuit of society portrait commissions. After Dodge had completed the portrait of George Pullman, Mrs. Pullman entered the room and offered her amateur criticism, obliging the artist to make changes against his better judgment. More disastrous was his experience painting Pullman's daughter, who was so displeased with her portrait that she threatened to destroy the work if changes were not made.[56] Furthermore, critical reaction to this show was less than flattering; one writer claimed that Dodge's color was "jarring" and his delivery "pretentious."[57] Several of the works found above reproach included Dodge's portrayal of his mother and that of his son Roger, described as charming; and the portrait of Carrère which was said to possess character and dignity. If Dodge had had any serious plans to pursue a career as a portrait painter however, they were soon abandoned.[58]

Although Dodge was not to make his mark as a society

Fig. 13
Sunken Garden, Villa Francesca, circa 1915, oil on panel, 31 x 36 inches.
Collection of Ursula and Leftwich Dodge Kimbrough

Fig. 14
Villa Francesca, circa 1906

portraitist, and had not yet received proper due for his other easel paintings, he had firmly established himself as a mural painter, and lucrative commissions steadily came his way. Shortly after he arrived in New York in 1900, he was offered $5000 to paint twenty-six decorative panels for the Café Martin, and by 1903 he was reported to be one of "our most successful artists, artistically and financially."[59] Flush with additional commissions he had received to decorate a wall in the cafe of the Hotel Algonquin, and to paint two lunettes and a mosaic ceiling design for the Hall of Records and Surrogate Court in New York, Dodge decided to build a country home for his family. He was thirty-nine years old, and after spending most of his life traveling between Europe and the United States, he wanted a more stable existence. Furthermore, as one writer observed, "although he has lived abroad for the greater portion of his lifetime, he is a true American in spirit."[60] It was time for Dodge to reestablish his roots in America and solidify his identity as an American artist.

In 1906, he designed and built Villa Francesca with the assistance of an engineer. This elaborate house, named in honor of his wife Fanny, was intended as a surprise for her and the children. For months Dodge traveled to various spots along the coast of Connecticut and Long Island before settling on the site he chose for his home, the dramatic sand bluffs overlooking Smithtown Bay, about fifty miles east of New York. Its proximity to the city was an important consideration, as he intended to maintain his studio there where he could easily obtain models to pose for his mural designs, and utilize another large studio on the estate to work up the actual murals from the sketches made in the city. The positioning of the house was crucial so that there would be a different effect every evening as the setting sun reflected off the water on the bay. The house itself was a rare blend of classical motifs and modern technology comprised of ornate porches, balconies, and porticos constructed of cement blocks. Shortly after completion, it was described as "a bit of ancient Greece set down on the shore of Long Island Sound."[61] Dodge based elements of the structure on actual Greek architecture, such as the Erectheum, creating an imposing sight, similar in opulence to Laurelton Hall, Louis Comfort Tiffany's Long Island estate. Built further west on the Sound in Oyster Bay in 1904 at a cost of $200,000, Tiffany's home, when completely decorated and landscaped in 1910, was valued at $2,000,000. Although it is doubtful that Dodge's expenses were anywhere near Tiffany's, they were certainly substantial.

Based on views of Villa Francesca painted by Dodge and contemporary photographs, there is no question of its splendor or breathtaking setting, neither of which went unnoticed by the press. In fact, one writer, Gustav Kobbe, provided a personally guided tour in an article written for the <u>New York Herald</u> in 1910. This account includes descriptions that enhance the appreciation of Dodge's paintings. The Kobbe "tour" began as one approached the house from the rear, entering through an elaborate concrete and iron gate: "Running one hundred and fifty feet along the cliff or bluff is

FIG. 15
The Atrium at Villa Francesca, circa 1906

a pergola of Ionic columns. The pergola is open at the center, leaving a space for a walk to the house, and at either side, where the pergola is cut through, are large Pompeian vases. A flight of broad marble steps has beautiful balustrades of white Greek marble in the design of the Italian Renaissance at the edge of the steps."[62]

Dodge's painting *Dolphin Bay*, 1913 (Plate 6), provides a glimpse of this scene, the artist's intent being to capture the evocative effects of the setting sun as it is reflected off the waters of what in actuality is Smithtown Bay and the snow-covered grounds of his estate. In what may be easily considered one of Dodge's most successful compositions, he utilizes merely a portion of the pergola to set off his asymmetrical design with its high horizon and flattened space, influenced by his interest in Japanese prints and the art of James McNeill Whistler. His carefully selected viewpoint is not chosen to feature the expansive sweep of the architectural structure as described by this writer, but to maximize on the decorative effect of the vertical elements provided by the posts, columns, and trees as they so perfectly punctuate his composition. As a muralist, Dodge was an expert in filling space in a decorative manner, a quality recognized by his critics and often used as high praise for his easel paintings.

Continuing the guided tour, Kobbe described entering the atrium of the house: "White marble paves the floor of the atrium, with a mosaic border in Greek fret of black and yellow. In the center is a beautiful fountain. The bowl is five by four feet and about a foot deep. It is made of Venetian glass mosaic — turquoise blue with a border of ultramarine blue and gold, forming an exquisite color spot in the center of the white marble. Rising from the bowl is a shaft of mosaic, and standing on it is a replica in bronze by Frederick MacMonnies of his *Pan of Rohallion* (back cover), with an inscription to Mr. Dodge."[63] The elaborate details of this splendid setting can be seen in *Atrium in Spring*, circa 1915 (Plate 9), including the MacMonnies *Pan of Rohallion*. Upon hearing from Dodge about the villa, MacMonnies sent him a cast of his popular bronze from Paris. Dodge, was delighted by its personal inscription and an accompanying note: "Your situation on the bluffs and ocean [Long Island Sound] and all must be heavenly and I envy you."[64] MacMonnies also commented facetiously: " I suppose you have millions in the bank."[65]

Also in the atrium stood an antique statue of Venus seen in both *Atrium in Spring* and *Venus in Atrium*, (The Metropolitan Museum of Art, Plate 5). It should be noted, however, that in his paintings, Dodge was not intent on providing a literal depiction of his opulent house; instead he

PLATE 5
Venus in Atrium, oil on canvas, 39¼ x 30 inches. The Metropolitan Museum of Art, Gift of Mr. and Mrs. Leftwich Dodge Kimbrough, 1972

PLATE 6
Dolphin Bay, circa 1913, oil on canvas, 44½ x 39¾ inches. Collection of Ursula and Leftwich Dodge Kimbrough

PLATE 7
Sunrise at East Hampton, oil on canvas, 35¼ x 45¾ inches

used the setting as a means of inspiration for his art. In each of the two works, he created a very comfortable, cloistered kind of space in which beautiful colors, combined in an almost cloisonné-like fashion, play off brilliant passages of dappled light. A great part of the appeal of these views of Dodge's home is inherent in their very personal and intimate nature, particularly the interiors that focus on the warmth of the home as seen through the eyes of its owner and creator.

"From the atrium one goes up by marble steps to a very large hall that rises straight to the roof of the house and has galleries around it, upon which open the rooms on the floor above," Kobbe continued. "To the right of this hall is the parlor and to the left the dining room, and an agreeable feature is secured by having the windows in the dining room open into the atrium, as well as outside; and both rooms have deep bay windows with seats."[66] Dodge obviously spared no expense in the embellishment of his interiors. The dining room was finished in carved antique oak paneling and oak rafters, with a dull blue painted ceiling. The color scheme of the parlor was gold and blue, its ceiling decorated with coffers having rosettes in the Romanesque style. The chandelier was in the style of the First Empire, while the mantel, mirror, and

FIG. 16
Sara and Aunt Katy, 1907, oil on canvas, 48 x 34¼ inches

furniture were "real old red and gold Louis XIV."[67] A view of the lush interior of the parlor is provided in Dodge's painting *Drawing Room* (Plate 10). As this painting indicates, Dodge was equally interested in the play of light off the highly reflective surfaces, such as the mirror, the marble column flanking the door, and the polished furniture and wood floor. He also captured the rich textural qualities of other furnishings such as the oriental carpets.

Unquestionably, Dodge would have been aware of, and inspired by, the luxuriant interiors painted by the American expatriate artist Walter Gay, who made this subject his specialty and prospered by portraying the interior spaces of his wealthy patrons' homes. There is no indication, however, that Dodge had any particular ambition along these lines; nor did he use these paintings in the manner of William Merritt Chase who widely exhibited views of his beautiful country home and studio in Shinnecock Hills (on the southeastern fork of Long Island) to display his success as a genteel painter.

Dodge exhibited easel paintings only intermittently in major annual exhibitions. The last paintings he contributed to such annual shows were based on several trips he made to Georgia between 1905 and 1907. In 1907 he contributed *Georgia (Live Oak at Sunset,* Plate 8), an evocative, tonal landscape, to the Pennsylvania Academy's annual exhibition. This work was also shown at the Paris Salon of 1907 under the title *Souvenir de Georgia.* Two other entries to the 1907 Paris Salon were family portraits: *Sara and Aunt Katy (Sarah et Tante Katy,* Fig. 16) also done during one of his trips to Georgia; and *Portrait of My Son Roger (Portrait de mon fils Roger).* Although the motivation for trips to Georgia is unclear, according to family history the Dodges were visiting a friend, Lily Livingston. *Summer Day Under Spanish Moss* (Greenville County Museum of Art, Fig. 2) was most likely painted near Savannah during one of these visits, as was *Sara and Aunt Katy,* portraying the artist's daughter with presumably one of Lily's servants. *Woods with Hanging Moss,* a watercolor, was also painted during one of these trips.

Dodge ultimately realized the debt he had incurred from his ambitious project in building Villa Francesca. And rather than making a special effort to sell his easel paintings to raise much needed funds, he turned instead to book illustration, teaching, and his most lucrative pursuit, mural painting. Most welcome news arrived in 1914. Dodge's friend, the painter Jules Guerin, informed Dodge that he had been awarded a $25,000 commission to paint two large mural panels (15 by 100 feet) for the entranceway to the Panama-Pacific Exposition to be held in San Francisco in 1915. These murals,

PLATE 8
Georgia (Live Oak at Sunset), circa 1907, oil on canvas, 40 x 30 inches

PLATE 9
Atrium in Spring, circa 1915, oil on canvas, 48 x 32 inches

PLATE 10
Drawing Room, Villa Francesca, circa 1916, oil on canvas, 35 x 27 inches

FIG. 17
Crane Neck Point, Winter, circa 1914, oil on canvas, 21¼ x 40 inches. Private Collection

which Dodge completed in his Setauket studio, were destined to adorn the "Tower of Jewels" designed by the architectural firm of Carrère and Hastings. Furthermore, Dodge was invited, along with the other artists working on murals for the fair, to take part in an exhibition of their easel paintings at the Palace Hotel in San Francisco which would precede the fair. Among the ten artists who took part in this exhibition were Frank Vincent DuMond, Frederick Childe Hassam, Robert Reid, and Edward Simmons, all known for their Impressionist paintings.[68] The other participants were mainly muralists.

The San Francisco exhibition provided an excellent opportunity for Dodge to display his recent works along with those by other notable painters. The show was ambitious in scale, numbering eighty-four works; Dodge contributed fifteen paintings, matched in quantity only by DuMond. Included in his selection were figure paintings and landscapes, mainly done at Villa Francesca. The exhibition, intended as a publicity tool for the upcoming fair, was so well received that it traveled to the Portland Museum in Oregon. Critics considered it to be a showcase of American Impressionism, with nothing "freakish or rabid" on display (undoubtedly a reference to the recent 1913 Armory show of Modern art held in New York and Chicago which shocked the general public).[69] Hassam, the best known of the group, was hailed as "one of the fathers of American Impressionism;"[70] and the

others were similarly praised for their contributions to what was described as the "most notable collection of work ever shown in San Francisco."[71]

Among the works by Dodge singled out for praise were a nocturne, *Coming of Night*, and three other paintings, *Innocence*, a nude bathed in sunlight, *Day Dreams*, and *My Pergola*, cumulatively described by one writer as filled with "sunlight and youth and roses, with a hint of the sea."[72] Also featured were two of Dodge's best winter scenes, *Dolphin Bay, Winter* and *Crayn's* [sic] *Neck, Winter* (Fig. 17). Unlike William Merritt Chase and Childe Hassam who focused on the summer months they spent at their country homes on Long Island, Dodge provided a full spectrum of seasonal views from Villa Francesca and its surrounding area. In fact, his serene winter scenes with their tonal colors were among the paintings most highly praised by contemporary critics. Although it would be difficult to characterize specific works by the other artists based only on their titles, it is evident that Hassam showed Impressionistic views of Cape Ann, Old Lyme, the Isles of Shoals, and East Hampton. Robert Reid contributed the female figure pieces with flowers for which he was best known, and Edward Simmons provided a small selection of female figure paintings and landscapes. Dodge's work was of a similar style and sentiment and was shown to full advantage.

When Dodge's mural paintings were unveiled at the

opening of the Panama-Pacific Exposition they were highly praised, even more so than the work of several of his colleagues. While Dodge and other painters known primarily as muralists received high accolades, Hassam and Reid, established easel painters, suffered attack. Eugene Neuhaus in <u>The Art of the Exposition</u> (1915) said of Reid: "The very scattered style of painting so effective in many of his easel paintings, which show all the fine qualities of a modern impressionist school, is not of great help in pictures intended to be viewed from a great distance."[73] Similarly, he criticized Hassam, claiming: "Nobody ever suspected Childe Hassam of being a decorator, no matter how admittedly important a place he holds in the field of easel painting."[74] In contrast to Hassam's coloring, which Neuhaus condemned as being "insipid," he found Dodge's to be "fine and lively," the decorations of a "most experienced artist treating a wide variety of interrelated subjects with great skill."[75]

Undoubtedly there was some prejudice against the easel painters, a prejudice Dodge, better known for his murals, often experienced in reverse when he exhibited his easel paintings, described by some critics as being too bold in color and too broad in brushwork. In fact, such commentary was mainly based on the bias of the critics, since Dodge's Impressionist paintings are, indeed, very similar to those of Reid and Hassam. Dodge's painting *Sally Among the Irises* (Plate 14), for example, might easily be compared to Reid's painting *Fleur de Lis* (The Metropolitan Museum of Art), probably painted in the late 1890s, and widely reproduced in articles and books shortly afterward. It was for paintings like this, in which Reid combined young female figures and flowers in a decorative manner, that he became best known. Although Dodge did not make this subject his signature theme, it is one he clearly and successfully addressed in his painting *Sally Among the Irises*. The emphasis in this work is on the play of strong reflected sunlight creating an overall pattern and flat decorative scheme, almost like a stained glass window.

Whereas many of Dodge's garden scenes feature a prominent figure, which is natural since his basic academic training was in figure painting, others are pure landscapes. Included among these is his watercolor *Crane Neck Point* (Fig. 18), near his home in Setauket. In this work, Dodge boldly focuses on a limited space. Its dramatic cropping, with only a slight indication of sky and little foreground, is reminiscent of Childe Hassam's paintings of the Isles of Shoals. Interestingly enough, while some critics credited this candid, cropped image as being "modern" and impressionistic when considering the work of artists like Hassam, they identified the same element in Dodge's paintings to be an extension of his decorative mural paintings. As a result, instead of being grouped with the emerging American Impressionists, with whom his easel paintings were closely aligned, he continued to be associated with the more conservative mural painters.

Closely following the success of the joint show held in San Francisco and Portland, and the extremely positive response Dodge was getting for his murals on view at the Panama-Pacific Exposition, was a one-man show held in New York in February 1915. This exhibition, held at the Folsom Galleries, included thirty-five paintings representing a wide array of subjects and styles, as well as studies for his murals at the Panama-Pacific Exposition. Dodge had every right to assume that this exhibition, including many paintings which received favorable comment when shown on the West Coast, would generate a positive response from New York art critics. For the most part this proved to be true; however, some critics were once again confused by the variety and diversity of Dodge's work. While several writers praised his tonal landscapes, *Dolphin Bay* being a particular favorite, most could not accept his Impressionistic garden scenes. Viewed in relation to his other

FIG. 18
Crane Neck Point, circa 1914, watercolor on paper, 20 x 14 inches

FIG. 19
Before the Ball, Villa Francesca, 1928, gouache and pencil on paper,
18½ x 13 inches. Private Collection

1929) where he offered various classes in illustration, perspective, life drawing, and composition. His elegant style and facility for painting figures — seen in his watercolor *Before the Ball*, 1928 (originally titled *Day After Ball*, Fig. 19) — always insured him work as an illustrator, while his teaching of perspective and composition inspired him to develop further his own keen skills along these lines. With the onset of World War I, Dodge's friend MacMonnies was forced to leave France and return to America. He visited Dodge in Setauket and they, undoubtedly, reminisced about their early years in Paris. Perhaps this was one factor that motivated Dodge to travel to France after the war in the fall of 1918. His primary mission, however, was to compose a series of major paintings commemorating important battles of the war as well as the peace treaty at Versailles. He worked on studies for his paintings in Paris, Versailles, and Verdun — where he sketched life drawings of French soldiers and German prisoners for his painting *The Battle of Verdun*. The results of this work met with limited success. Based on his concern for detail and accu-

works which were much more subdued, these paintings were considered overbearing. While one critic acknowledged Dodge as "pre-eminently a painter of sunshine," he preferred the harmonious nocturnes in the exhibition.[76] Another criticized Dodge's Impressionistic garden scenes as being: "uncompromisingly direct...too eager, too vigorous, to care much for nuances of tone."[77] Fortunately, more enlightened critics extolled the same paintings for their brilliant color, one describing these works as "arresting and full of the spirit of gayety [sic]."[78] Others responded positively to the personal content of the works which were, for the most part, based on the artist's tranquil domestic life at his country home. Nearly all commented on the decorative nature of Dodge's paintings, not necessarily in a pejorative way. Dodge was, indeed, a muralist who devoted much of his concern to "filling up space" in a well-designed manner. Responding to such comments, Dodge stated: "I hope my work is decorative. If it is decorated a tenth as well as nature does, I should be completely satisfied."[79]

In 1915 Dodge began teaching, first at the Art Students League (1915, 1925-29), and then at Cooper Union (1916-

FIG. 20
Sara Pryor Dodge at Villa Francesca, 1928

PLATE 11
Villa de Leftwich, circa 1926, gouache and pencil on paper, 22 x 15 inches

racy, learned from his master, Gérôme, Dodge portrayed the foreign delegates in *The Signing of the Peace, Versailles* (1919) in their native costumes instead of the suits they wore — as a result, the committee in charge of selecting paintings for the project rejected Dodge's 16 by 26-foot painting. It was obvious that Dodge could not give up the idea of painting grandly scaled Salon-type works which had long since become outdated.

During this trip to France, Dodge also completed more successful, smaller-scale, easel paintings, such as *Hall of Mirrors, Versailles*. This work in its conception, tonality, and concern for light is similar to paintings by John Singer Sargent. Its dramatic perspective and unusual vantage point also reflect Dodge's experience as a mural painter and teacher of composition. A comparison to the work of Sargent can also be made in several watercolors painted by Dodge on subsequent trips to Europe and to Mexico. In 1926 he visited his mother who had settled in a villa just outside of Rome which she renamed "Villa de Leftwich." Dodge completed at least one watercolor of the villa (Plate 11) in which he focused on the effects of strong light and shadow, and the patterns they

FIG. 21
Temple of Neptune, Paestum, circa 1926,
gouache and pencil on paper, 19¼ x 14 inches

created. This watercolor reveals Dodge's growing concern for perspective as seen in the broad empty space of the diagonal path that leads the viewer dramatically into the picture plane. During this trip, Dodge also visited southern Italy and Sicily where he painted watercolors of the ancient ruins. These watercolors provided the basis for his next one-man show, "Watercolors of Greek Temples in Sicily," held at the Milch Galleries in New York, January 30-February 11, 1928. Among the works featured was *Temple of Neptune, Paestum* (Fig. 21), composed in his usual direct manner with the columns of the temple thrust dramatically into the foreground. This imposing vantage point is one he had used successfully as a mural painter and now had perfected as a watercolorist.

Early in 1928, Dodge suffered a heart attack. The period had been very trying for him. Around 1921 he had purchased and began renovating a townhouse at 52 West 9th Street which he expected to finance with proceeds from a commission to execute murals for the "Flag Room" of the New York State Capital in Albany. At the time, Dodge was reported to be the highest-paid muralist in the country, with his fee based on the square footage of the job. The advance fee he was to receive for this mural project was $42,000.[50] Because of delays due to state politics, it was not until 1928 that he got approval to complete the project and, presumably, got paid. The strenuous project was then completed with the assistance of his daughter. In October, his mother Mamie died in Italy.

At year's end, he was given another one-man exhibition at Milch Galleries, "Water Colors of Architectural Subjects in France/ Also Landscape and Figures by William de Leftwich Dodge," November 19-December 1, 1928. Most likely, the first Milch show in January/February of 1928 was so successful it prompted a second exhibition. An annotated catalogue for the November/December show provides some insight into the price scale — $250 to $500, certainly respectable for the time. Among the highest-priced works were: *Chateau Fontainebleau*; *Carrouselle* [sic] *Arch, Tuilleries* (*Le Carrousel du Louvre*, Fig. 24); and *Deck of the SS De Grasse* (Plate 12), all listed at $500. Two special works on loan (not for sale) were *Day After Ball*, lent by the artist's daughter Sara, and *Gathering Dogwood* - most likely a Long Island scene. A related work, *Pink Dogwood, Mill Neck*, was praised in a review in The New York Times for its "brilliant effects of local color."[51]

Deck of the SS De Grasse and *Swash of the Steamer*, two very different works, were done while Dodge was crossing the Atlantic Ocean. The first of these watercolors is a detailed view of the ship's deck, and Dodge's main concern of rendering the effect of light and shadow is clearly evident. In

PLATE 12
Deck of the S.S. De Grasse, circa 1926, gouache and pencil on paper, 19¾ x 14¼ inches

PLATE 13
Tiger Lilies, circa 1925, oil on canvas, 48 x 32 inches. Collection of Kathleen Kaye-McKean and David McKean

PLATE 14

Sally Among the Irises, circa 1906, oil on canvas, 32 x 20 inches

contrast, the second watercolor of bounding waves of the open sea relates to oil paintings made during previous journeys. Included in the show were opulent interior views of Villa Francesca, also similar to previous works in oil but freer in execution, with broad swaths of light and shadow painted in the style of John Singer Sargent.

Regardless of any money Dodge might have realized from the sale of watercolors from these exhibitions, he knew that the underpinning of his finances was his mural work. In 1929, in spite of poor health, he traveled to Lynchburg, Virginia, to oversee the installation of his mural for the Baptist Hospital. The following year, he undertook what would be his most ambitious and successful private commission, completing a series of highly praised allegorical murals, *Europe Through the Ages*, for the Manhattan residence of Arthur Brisbane, noted newspaper editor. For relaxation, and because he had a great interest in ancient cultures, Dodge traveled during the summer of 1930 with his wife and daughter to Mexico, where he painted a series of watercolors of the Mayan ruins. A selection of these works was exhibited at the Brooklyn Museum and later featured in another solo show at Milch Galleries,

FIG. 22
Ezell's Brother, 1933, gouache and pencil on paper, 20 x 14 inches

"William de Leftwich Dodge/Watercolors of Yucatan, 'Land of the Mayas,'" December 7-19, 1931.

Dodge's interest in the ancient civilizations of Central America can be traced back to Paris in the 1890s when he worked on a grand-scale painting titled *The Conquest of Mexico*, shown at the Salon of 1899. By the time Dodge visited Mexico in 1930, he was convinced that there was a lost continent in the Pacific that had originally linked Asia and the Americas, basing this belief on the similarity of the Khmer sculpture of Cambodia and the art of the Mayas. Whether or not there was any scientific evidence for this theory, it did help generate publicity for the exhibition in reviews, like one titled "Mayan Art Bears out Myth of Lost Continent," published in the New York Sun.[52] The show consisted of twenty-six watercolors, mainly ancient ruins which evidently had become a favorite subject in this medium. Watercolor itself was less taxing than oil painting, and, of course, more suited to travel, especially in torrid climates. Two years later, ten of these "Mexican" watercolors, along with the eight by fifteen-foot Salon painting, *The Conquest of Mexico* (Tulane University), were displayed at the Chicago World's Fair of 1933.

During the family trip to Mexico, Dodge's daughter Sara had met Hunter Southworth Kimbrough, descended from an old Mississippi family, who would soon afterward become her husband. Shortly after their marriage, Dodge visited the couple in Greenwood, Mississippi, in 1933. On this trip he painted several Southern subjects including his watercolor, *Ezell's Brother* (Fig. 22), a forceful rendition of an elderly man in which Dodge focused almost exclusively on the model's strong character, developing little more than his facial features, set against an almost abstract background.

At the height of the Depression in December 1933, Dodge sent a note to Juliana Force in an unsuccessful attempt to get work for himself through the Government's Public Works of Art Project. "I do not aspire to do any mural painting as that work I suppose will be given to the younger and more modern men," he wrote.[53] He did hope, however, to supervise the color scheme of some project, having served this function at the Sesqui-Centennial Exposition (1926) in Philadelphia. Dodge had also been commissioned to do designs for the New York Public Library (a project that never materialized) and for a mural at West Point.[54] The following year, 1934, Dodge exhibited what would be his last entry in the Paris Salon, *Madonna of the Oleanders*. Obviously this was of significance to him personally, even though by this point such exhibitions were considered "passé" by most other serious artists. The work depicted a young deaf mute girl who had

FIG. 23
Low Tide, Port Jefferson, 1928, gouache and pencil on paper, 14 x 19¼ inches

picked flowers from the garden of Villa de Leftwich to be placed at a shrine to the Madonna. Although sentimental in nature, it appropriately marked the end of a career that had begun in Paris nearly fifty years before, when he had his first work accepted for the spring Salon of 1887. In 1901, early in Dodge's career, the art critic Sadakichi Hartmann, who had been a supporter of his work, described Dodge as "a young aspirant to fame, who considers a first class medal the Alpha and Omega of art, and applies the usual Salon methods of painting colossal canvasses [sic] to obtain it."[85] This astute observation might have served as a fitting epitaph for Dodge who died March 25, 1935, just a year after exhibiting his final painting at the Paris Salon.

Epilogue

It is unfortunate that William de Leftwich Dodge's reputation as an easel painter was overshadowed early in his career by the grand-scale, elaborate exhibition pieces for the Paris Salon, and later by his celebrity as a mural painter. His versatility, painting in a wide range of styles and diverse subject matter, proved to be confusing to critics trying to

assign an identity to his work. Furthermore, his Impressionist easel paintings with their vivid colors and bold brushwork were too overpowering and advanced for most critics. In describing the easel paintings of Dodge's colleague Robert Reid, also an important muralist, Sadakichi Hartmann referred to his style as "decorative impressionism,"[86] — no doubt a comment on the amalgamation of formal decorative elements inherent in mural design with the high key and more fluid aspects of Impressionism. In fact, this term could be applied to paintings by other American Impressionists, such as Childe Hassam and Edward Simmons, also muralists. And certainly the term is appropriate for many of the paintings by Dodge. From his subtle, tonal landscapes and evocative marines to his brilliant, sun-filled garden scenes and luminous watercolors, Dodge brought to his work a keen understanding of design and "decoration" — a term he was proud to have applied to his paintings.

Ronald G. Pisano
April 1998

32   The Author would like to acknowledge the following for their important contributions to this essay: H. Barbara Weinberg, Curator of Painting and Sculpture, The Metropolitan Museum of Art; Ita Berkow, Curator of Art, Museums at Stony Brook; Deborah Johnson, President, Museums at Stony Brook; Robert B. MacKay, Director, Society for the Preservation of Long Island Antiquities; Barbara van Liew, Society for the Preservation of Long Island Antiquities; Wendy Kail; David Cassedy; D. Frederick Baker; George Kuper; William H. Gerdts; and Jeffrey Boys.

[1] The New York Times, March 26, 1935, p. 20.

[2] Sara Dodge Kimbrough, Drawn from Life, (Jackson, MS: University of Mississippi Press, 1976) p. 171.

[3] Truth, March, 1901, p. 55.

[4] Unless otherwise noted, all biographical information was drawn from Sara Dodge Kimbrough, Drawn from Life (Jackson, MS: University of Mississippi Press, 1976) and Frederick Platt, "A Brief Autobiography of William de Leftwich Dodge," The American Art Journal, Spring, 1982, pp. 55-63. The first source, written by the artist's daughter, is not always reliable, and the sources for her information are not credited; however, it is the only major source of personal information. Platt's article is a finely edited version of a short autobiographical account written by Dodge himself. According to family sources, Dodge's mother Mary changed her maiden name from Leftwich to de Leftwich, based upon her discovery of tombstones marked "de Leftwich" in an English cemetary of her ancestors, a change adopted by William for his middle name around 1890.

[5] "William de Leftwich Dodge/American Painter of Distinction," Fine Arts Journal, XIV, No. 2, February, 1903, p. 44.

[6] Classes at the Ecole, the state school, were free, even for foreign students. Colarossi, a private school administered by the Italian sculptor, Filippo Colarossi, charged a small fee.

[7] Richard Whiteing, "The American Student at the Beaux-Arts," The Century Magazine, December, 1881, p. 262. For further information on Gérôme students, see: H. Barbara Weinberg, The American Pupils of Jean-Leon Gérôme , Fort Worth, TX: Amon Carter Museum, 1984.

[8] Mary Smart, A Flight with Fame/The Life and Art of Frederick MacMonnies, Madison, CT: Soundview Press, 1996, p. 44. MacMonnies notes (Nov. 1884) that he and several other art students, including James F. Brown and George Gray Barnard, met at Dodge's studio to decide what to do. Dodge and Barnard were already packed to leave for Berlin; MacMonnies and Brown later left for Munich. For Dodge's early association with MacMonnies and other American art students, see this source.

[9] Kimbrough, p. 6.

[10] Kimbrough, p. 13.

[11] "Painter and Sculptor Estimated by his Famous American Pupils: J. Alden Weir, Douglas Volk and William Leftwich [sic] Dodge." Unidentified news clipping, written at the time of Gérôme's death in 1904, Dodge Papers, courtesy of Leftwich Dodge Kimbrough.

[12] Ibid.

[13] Ibid.

[14] Ibid.

[15] Whiteing, pp. 265-66.

[16] Whiteing, p. 266. For a detailed study on American students at the Ecole, see: H. Barbara Weinberg, "Nineteenth-Century American Painters at the Ecole des Beaux-Arts," The American Art Journal, 13, Autumn, 1981, pp. 66-84.

[17] For details on this subject, I am indebted to: Cynthia D. Nickerson, "Artistic Interpretations of Henry Wadsworth Longfellow's The Song of Hiawatha, 1855-1900," The American Art Journal, Summer, 1984, pp. 49-77.

[18] Unidentified and undated news clipping, Dodge papers.

[19] For detailed treatment of this subject, see: Lois Marie Fink, American Art at the Nineteenth- Century Paris Salons, Cambridge: Cambridge University Press, 1990.

[20] See: Annette Blaugrund, Paris 1889/American Artists at the Universal Exposition, New York: Pennsylvania Academy of the Fine Arts, Philadelphia, and Harry N. Abrams, Inc., 1989. Blaugrund notes Rosalie Gill's birth date might have been the same as Dodge (1867), but that has not been confirmed.

[21] Dodge showed his paintings infrequently and erratically in such exhibitions: showing at the NAD only once (1890); at the AIC (1893, 1895, and 1898); and at the PAFA irregularly (between 1891 and 1907). For a full analytical discussion of Dodge's easel paintings, see: Frederick Platt, "The Easel Paintings of William de Leftwich Dodge," 19th Century, Spring, 1990, pp. 7-10.

[22] 1. The Burial of Minnesink (Salon 1889); 2. David (Salon 1888); 3. The Death of Minnehaha (Gold Medal, American Art Association, 1887); 4. Water Lilies. Girl in Sunlight (Salon 1889); 5. Girl After the Bath (Munich Exhibition 1888).

[23] Jules Bastien-Lepage was highly regarded by American artists, particularly those working in France; and his painting Joan of Arc was much celebrated and had a major impact on the work of Dodge and others. Dodge's painting The Death of Minnehaha had already been compared to it in the American press.

[24] Dodge's asymmetrical design in Sunset with its high horizon line suggests a familiarity with the work of James McNeill Whistler and Japanese prints.

[25] Agnes Farley Miller, "Fine Arts/The Paris Salon," The Independent, March 5, 1891, p. 791.

[26] Charles Henry Hart, "The Pennsylvania Academy Exhibition," The Independent, March 5, 1891, p. 342.

[27] For a fuller discussion, see: Marjorie Balge, "William de Leftwich Dodge: American Renaissance Artist," Art & Antiques, January-February, 1982, pp. 95-103. Balge also discusses other mural projects and was among the first to deal with Dodge's easel paintings.

[28] Unidentified and undated news clipping, Dodge Papers.

[29] Unidentified and undated news clipping, Dodge Papers.

[30] Unidentified and undated news clipping, Dodge Papers.

[31] For a full discussion, see: Leftwich Dodge Kimbrough, "Portrait of the Artist/Dodge's Murals Helped Create 'National Monument of Art,'" Library of Congress Information Bulletin, May 5-19, 1997, pp. 174-78.

[32] "Paintings by American," The New York Times, February 21, 1897, p. 5.

[33] Ibid.

[34] "Sale of Dodge Paintings," The New York Times, February 24, 1897, p. 7.

[35] "A Day's Wedding/Dodge —Prior," The New York Times, April 1, 1897, p. 3.

[36] Smart, p. 188.

[37] Will H. Low, Chronicle of Friendship, New York: Scribner's Sons, 1908, p. 446.

[38] Ibid.

[39] Low, p. 449.

[40] Ibid.

[41] Low, pp. 448-449.

[42] For a full discussion of this subject, see: William H. Gerdts, Monet's Giverny/An Impressionist Colony, New York: Abbeville Press, 1993.

[43] Georgia Fraser Arkell, "The Paintings of William de Leftwich Dodge," Art Education, February, 1901, pp. 242-46.

[44] J. Herbert Welch, "A Painter of Promise and Achievement," Truth, March, 1901, pp. 55-58.

[45] Arkell, p. 242.

[46] Arkell, p. 244.

[47] Chicago Chronicle, February 1, 1901, news clipping, Dodge Papers, page unknown.

[48] Unidentified news clipping, January 29, 1901, Dodge Papers.

[49] James William Pattison, "Fuss about Dodge's Nudes," unidentified news clipping, Dodge Papers.

[50] Chicago Times Herald, February 3, 1901, news clipping, Dodge Papers, page unknown.

[51] Chicago News, January 29, 1901, news clipping, Dodge Papers, page unknown.

[52] Pattison, page unknown.

[53] Arkell, p. 244; 246.

[54] "William de Leftwich Dodge/American Painter of Distinction," p. 48.

[55] Ibid.

[56] Kimbrough, pp. 38-39.

[57] "Art and Artists/Portraits by William de Leftwich Dodge — Pictures Forgeries," unidentified news clipping (Archives of American Art, New York, Reel 379, No. 835).

[58] Ibid.

[59] "William de Leftwich Dodge/American Painter of Distinction," p. 48.

[60] Ibid.

[61] Gustave Kobbe, "Ancient Greece Reproduced in Long Island Villa," New York Herald, Magazine Section, August 14, 1910, p. 11.

[62] Ibid.

[63] Ibid.

[64] Kimbrough, p. 5.

[65] Ibid.

[66] Kobbe, p. 11.

[67] Ibid.

[68] The other artists represented were: Milton H. Bancroft, Frank Brangwyn, Frederick Melville DuMond, Jules Guerin, and Charles Holloway.

[69] Unidentified news clipping, Dodge Papers.

[70] Ibid.

[71] Unidentified news clipping, Dodge Papers.

[72] Ward Winchell, "This Art Exhibit A Poem in Paint," unidentified news clipping, Dodge Papers.

[73] Eugene Neuhaus, The Art of the Exposition, San Francisco: Paul Elder & Co., 1915, pp. 56- 57.

[74] Neuhaus, p. 60.

[75] Neuhaus, p. 61.

[76] Unidentified news clipping, Dodge Papers.

[77] Unidentified news clipping, Dodge Papers.

[78] The New York Times, February 11, 1915, p. 8.

[79] Welch, p. 56.

[80] Kimbrough, p. 130.

[81] The New York Times, November 25, 1928, news clipping, Dodge Papers, page unknown.

[82] "Mayan Art Bears out Myth of Lost Continent: William de Leftwich Dodge Advances Theory Based on Similarity of Ornament Found in Yucatan and Cambodia," New York Sun, news clipping, Dodge Papers, date and page unknown.

[83] Letter from William de Leftwich Dodge to Juliana Force, December 14, 1933, Dodge Papers.

[84] Letter from William de Leftwich Dodge to Juliana Force, January 9, 1934, Dodge Papers.

[85] Sadakichi Hartmann, A History of American Art, vol. II, Boston: LC. Page and Company, 1901, pp. 191-92.

[86] Hartmann, p. 251.

FIG. 24

Le Carrousel du Louvre, circa 1926, gouache and pencil on paper, 20 x 14 inches

PLATE 15
Stepping in the Fountain, 1916, oil on canvas, 32 x 19 inches. National Museum of American Art

WILLIAM DE LEFTWICH DODGE
Chronology

1867   Born March 9 in Liberty (Bedford), Virginia, to Mary de Leftwich and William M. Dodge.

1870-8   Lives in Chicago, Illinois.

1879   Lives briefly in Brooklyn, New York, and then travels to Europe with his mother, his older sister Anita, and his younger brother Robert.

1880   Lives in Munich, Germany, while his mother studies art.

1881   Family moves to Paris.

1882   Dodge begins to study art at the Académie Colarossi and to attend classes at the Ecole Nationale des Beaux-Arts.

1883   Begins his studies in Jean-Léon Gérôme's studio.

1884   Family moves briefly to Berlin, where Dodge studies at the Königliche Akademische Hochschule.

1885   Returns to Paris and formally enrolls in the Ecole Nationale des Beaux-Arts; wins two third-place medals, two honorable mentions, and the Prix d'Atelier during the course of his studies with Gérôme.

1887   Exhibits a bas relief sculpture (*Portrait de Mlle xxx*) at the Paris Salon. Exhibits *The Death of Minnehaha* at the Prize Fund Exhibition in New York; receives one of ten gold medals awarded by the exhibiting artists.

1888   Exhibits his painting *David and Goliath* at the Paris Salon.

1889   Moves to New York and shares a small studio at 4 and 6 West 14th Street with George Bridgman. Becomes an illustrator for various magazines. Exhibits *The Burial of Minnesink* and *Woman in the Sun* at the Salon. Wins a bronze medal at the Exposition Universelle in Paris for *David and Goliath*.

FIG. 25
Sara Pryor Dodge at the Fountain, Villa Francesca, 1916

1890   Exhibits *Portrait of a Lady*, *A Study* and *Cascades de Cenery* [sic] at the National Academy. Joins Alexander Harrison and Charles Walter Stetson in a joint exhibition of their pictures at the American Art Galleries in New York.

1891   Travels to Chicago and paints a panorama of the Chicago Fire of 1871. Returns to New York after hearing that his studio has burned. Exhibits eight pictures at the Pennsylvania Academy of the Fine Arts, including *The Death of Minnehaha*. Dodge, Gilbert Gaul, and Frederick Remington share a commission to illustrate a series of articles in <u>Century Magazine</u> about California and the hunt for gold. Wins commission to paint the mural of the dome of Richard Morris Hunt's Administration Building at the Columbian Exposition.

1892　Auctions ninety-six of his pictures at the Fifth Avenue Art Galleries in New York. Returns to Chicago and has public dispute with Frank Millet (Director of Decorations) over personal expenses incurred due to a five and one-half month delay in completion of the dome before Dodge can begin his mural painting.

1893　Completes the dome mural with the help of his brother Robert and wins an Exposition award for his work.

1894　Returns to Paris.

1895　Accepts and begins important commission to paint murals for four tympanums and a dome ceiling at the Library of Congress in Washington, DC. Exhibits *The Dream of Orpheus* and *Sea at Sunset* at the Pennsylvania Academy. Also exhibits *Evening Dance* and *Diane* at the Paris Salon and four pictures at the annual exhibition at the Art Institute of Chicago.

1896　Finishes his Library of Congress murals and exhibits one section *L'Ambition* at the Paris Salon. Returns to New York and exhibits these decorations along with a number of easel paintings at the American Art Galleries.

1897　Auctions fifty-three pictures in New York. Installs decorative murals in the Library of Congress. Marries Frances Theodora Bland Pryor on March 31 and honeymoons in Saratoga Springs, New York. Several weeks later they move to Paris.

1898　Birth of the Dodges' son Roger Pryor Dodge. Exhibits *Orpheus Singing to the Animals* at the Pennsylvania Academy and *War* (*La Guerre*) at the Art Institute of Chicago and at the Paris Salon. Visits Algiers with Frederick MacMonnies and Paul Conkling. The Dodge family moves to Giverny and takes a house next door to MacMonnies.

1899　Exhibits *Princess Varda in the Bath* and *The Conquest of Mexico* at the Salon and *War* at the Pennsylvania Academy. Serves as primary illustrator of five-volume set titled *The Great Operas*.

1900　Returns to New York in December to execute magazine illustration commissions. Exhibits recent pictures at the American Art Galleries and works on a plan for an airplane/helicopter.

1901　Exhibits *La Sainte Ivresse* and a portrait of his wife and son at the Salon. Also has a one-man show of seventy works at the Art Institute of Chicago, including *Roger* (*Roger with Guitar*). Birth of Dodge's daughter Sara Pryor Dodge in July. Successfully tests a model airplane/helicopter that flies 25 feet in his studio in the Tenth Street Studio Building.

1902　Paints the drop curtain and six lunettes for the Majestic Theatre in Boston.

1903　Wins an injunction against the Allied Arts Company and Louis C. Tiffany prohibiting the alteration of murals that they contracted him to paint for the lobby of the King Edward Hotel in Toronto, Canada; Dodge later reports that the murals were repainted despite the court's ruling.

1904　Exhibits paintings and portraits at the Durand-Ruel Galleries in New York, including *My Family* (*Family Group*) and *Baby Roger* (*Roger with Guitar*). Also exhibits *La Sainte Ivresse* and a portrait of Mrs. Francis Carolan at the Louisiana Purchase Exposition in St. Louis.

1906　Exhibits *The Sea* and *Jeanette* at the Pennsylvania Academy. Builds Greek Revival style house, Villa Francesca, at Setauket, Long Island. Decorates the east wall of the cafe in the Hotel Algonquin. Completes two lunettes and a mosaic ceiling for the Hall of Records and Surrogate Court in New York.

1907　Exhibits portraits *Sarah et Tante Katy* and *Portrait de mon fils Roger* at the Paris Salon and *Georgia* at the Pennsylvania Academy. Illustrates *The Birth of the Nation*, his mother-in-law Sara Pryor's historical account of the establishment of the Virginia colony in Jamestown.

1908　Completes decoration and murals for the Brooklyn Academy of Music.

1914　Installs two decorative murals in the Court of Jewels in San Francisco for the Panama-Pacific

Exposition of 1915. Exhibits easel pictures at the Palace Hotel there and at the Portland Art Association in Oregon, including *Dolphin Bay* and *Crayn's* [sic] *Neck - Winter*. Completes murals for the Orpheum Theatre in Philadelphia.

1915   Teaches composition and perspective for one year at the Art Students League. Has a one-man show at the Folsom Galleries in New York.

1916   Begins teaching various classes in composition and illustration at Cooper Union (until 1929).

1918   Travels to Paris late in the year to paint several pictures commemorating important battles of the war and the peace treaty at Versailles; these include *They Shall Not Pass - Verdun, Belleau* and *The Signing of the Peace, Versailles, 1919*.

1920   Completes murals for library at State Teachers College, Cedar Falls, Iowa.

1921   Dodge's rooms in the Tenth Street Studio Building are ransacked during a burglary, and several canvases are stolen, including a portrait of the Earl of Albemarle and *The Fawn Dance*.

1924   Moves into his studio at 52 West Ninth Street around this time.

1925   Begins teaching various classes in composition, illustration, and life drawing at the Art Students League (until 1929).

1926   Serves as Chief of Color at the Sesqui-Centennial International Exposition in Philadelphia. Travels to Italy to visit his mother near Rome. Visits Sicily and southern Italy and paints watercolors of the Greek ruins there.

1928   Suffers heart attack in early part of the year. Exhibits the Greek watercolors at the Milch Galleries in New York and a portrait, *Captain Davis*, at the Corcoran Gallery of Art. Assisted by his daughter Sara, Dodge completes murals for the Flag Room of the State Capitol in Albany, New York. Dodge's mother dies in Italy in October. Exhibits more watercolors of France and Long Island at the Milch Galleries in November, including *Fountain of Medici, Deck of the S.S. De Grasse,*

and *Low Tide, Port Jefferson*. Also exhibits *Sun Bath* at the National Academy's Winter Exhibition.

1929   Despite continuing weakness from his earlier heart attack, he travels to Lynchburg, Virginia, to oversee the installation of his mural for the Baptist Hospital there.

1930   Travels to Mexico with his wife and daughter; paints a series of watercolors depicting Mayan ruins. Completes a series of allegorical murals for Arthur Brisbane's Manhattan residence, titled *Europe Through the Ages*, which the magazine *Architect* lavishly praises.

1931   Exhibits twenty-six of his watercolors of architecture of the Yucatan at the Brooklyn Museum and later at the Milch Galleries. Smithsonian Institution arranges with the artist to display the airplane/helicopter model that he had designed in 1901. Completes murals for the lobby of the Buffalo City Hall.

1933   Exhibits watercolors and oil paintings, including *Conquest of Mexico*, at the Chicago's World Fair. Designs a publicity poster to promote Sergei Eisenstein's *Thunder over Mexico*, a film financed through the assistance of Upton Sinclair and his wife who was Sara Dodge's sister-in-law. Works briefly on mural projects at West Point and the New York Public Library for the federally subsidized Public Works of Art Project.

1934   Exhibits *Madonna of the Oleanders* at the Paris Salon.

1935   Dies March 25 in New York.

Robert Bardin
April 1998

Fig. 26
Drawing Room, Villa Francesca, 1928, gouache and pencil on paper, 20 x 13¾ inches

Cover: *The Artist's Garden*, circa 1916, oil on canvas, 35 x 27 inches
Back Cover: Frederick MacMonnies, *Pan of Rohallion*, bronze, 30¼ inches high

Inside Front Cover: Corner of Villa Francesca, 1906
Inside Back Cover: Villa Francesca Looking Through the Foyer to the Dining Room, circa 1906

Title Page: Frederick MacMonnies, *Bacchante with Infant Faun*, bronze, dark brown patina, 16 inches high

© 1998 Beacon Hill Fine Art
Design: Gerngross & Company, New York City
Printing: Centennial Printing Corporation
Photography: Arturs Vitols, Helga Photo Studio